Inspirational Quotes

365 days of motivation and inspiration

Table of Contents

Introduction

Thank you for choosing this book, containing 365 inspirational quotes.

This book is designed to provide you with an inspirational quote for every single day of the year. However, it can really be used however you like!

You can choose to read a quote every morning to start off your day on the right foot, or you can simply flip this book open to a random page whenever you feel the need.

All 365 inspirational quotes have been hand-selected to help you to persevere, to feel positive, and to continue working towards your goals and dreams! Included are quotes from famous philosophers, activists, musicians, politicians, leaders, athletes, entrepreneurs, and more!

No matter how you choose to use this book, I hope that it provides you with inspiration, motivation, and joy, whenever you need it most.

365 Inspirational Quotes

1.

"The secret of getting ahead is getting started."

- Mark Twain

2.

"Magic is believing in yourself. If you can make that happen, you can make anything happen."

- Johann Wolfgang Von Goethe

3.

"We are what we repeatedly do. Excellence, then, is not an act, but a habit."

- Aristotle

4.

"If you believe it'll work out, you'll see opportunities. If you don't believe it'll work out, you'll see obstacles."

- Wayne Dyer

5.

"Don't be pushed around by the fears in your mind. Be led by the dreams in your heart."

- Roy T. Bennett

6.

"I hated every minute of training, but I said 'Don't quit. Suffer now and live the rest of your life as a champion'."

- Muhammad Ali

7.

"You must do the thing you think you cannot do."

- Eleanor Roosevelt

8.

"I never lose. Either I win or I learn."

- Nelson Mandela

9.

"Today is the opportunity to build the tomorrow you want."

- Ken Poirot

10.

"Doubt kills more dreams than failure ever will."

- Suzy Kassem

11.

"If you want to fly, give up everything that weighs you down."

- Buddha

12.

"You don't need to see the whole staircase, just take the first step."

- Martin Luther King Jr.

13.

"Be happy with what you have while working for what you want."

- Helen Keller

14.

"Be so good they can't ignore you."

-   Steve Martin

15.

"Do what you can, with what you have, where you are."

-   Theodore Roosevelt

16.

"It's never too late to be what you might've been."

-   George Eliot

17.

"You can do anything you set your mind to."

- Benjamin Franklin

18.

"Twenty years from now you'll be more disappointed by the things you did not do than the ones you did."

- Mark Twain

19.

"The world is full of nice people. If you can't find one, be one."

- Nishan Panwar

20.

"You can't go back and change the beginning, but you can start where you are and change the ending."

- C.S. Lewis

21.

"A winner is a dreamer who never gives up."

- Nelson Mandela

22.

"The question isn't who is going to let me; it's who is going to stop me."

- Ayn Rand

23.

"And, when you want something, all the universe conspires in helping you to achieve it."

- Paulo Coelho

24.

"We need to accept that we won't always make the right decisions, that we'll screw up royally sometimes – understanding that failure is not the opposite of success, it's part of success."

- Arianna Huffington

25.

"Doubt is a killer. You just have to know who you are and what you stand for."

- Jennifer Lopez

26.

"Be a first-rate version of yourself, not a second-rate version of someone else."

- Judy Garland

27.

"Learn from the mistakes from others. You can't live long enough to make them all yourself."

- Eleanor Roosevelt

28.

"If your dreams don't scare you, they are too small."

- Sir Richard Branson

29.

"A man is not finished when he is defeated. He is finished when he quits."

- Richard Nixon

30.

"Be the change you want to see in the world."

- Mahatma Gandhi

31.

"Be silly, be honest, be kind."

- Ralph Waldo Emerson

32.

"It's not what happens to you, but how you react to it that matters."

- Epictetus

33.

"Don't watch the clock; do what it does. Keep going."

- Sam Levenson

34.

"Work until your idols become rivals."

- Drake

35.

"Falling down is how we grow. Staying down is how we die."

- Brian Vaszily

36.

"There may be people that have more talent than you, but there's no excuse for anyone to work harder than you."

- Derek Jeter

37.

"Be an encourager. When you encourage others, you boost their self-esteem, enhance their self-confidence, make them work harder, lift their spirits and make them successful in their endeavors. Encouragement goes straight to the heart and is always available. Be an encourager. Always."

- Roy T. Bennett

38.

"You can control two things: your work ethic and your attitude about anything."

- Ali Krieger

39.

"Success isn't always about greatness. It's about consistency. Consistent hard work leads to success. Greatness will come."

- Dwayne 'The Rock' Johnson

40.

"Motivation comes from working on things we care about."

- Sheryl Sandberg

41.

"If today you are a little bit better than you were yesterday, then that's enough."

- David A. Bednar

42.

"Education is the most powerful weapon which you can use to change the world."

- Nelson Mandela

43.

"You may be disappointed if you fail, but you'll be doomed if you don't try."

- Beverly Sills

44.

"Failure is the tuition you pay for success."

- Walter Brunell

45.

"Study while others are sleeping; work while others are loafing; prepare while others are playing; and dream while others are wishing."

- William Arthur Ward

46.

"The best revenge is massive success."

- Frank Sinatra

47.

"It's never too late for a new beginning in your life."

- Joyce Meyers

48.

"Never doubt that a small group of thoughtful, committed citizens can change the world. Indeed, it is the only thing that ever has."

- Margaret Mead

49.

"Everyone thinks of changing the world, but no one thinks of changing himself."

- Leo Tolstoy

50.

"Don't give up, don't take anything personally, and don't take no for an answer."

- Sophia Amoruso

51.

"The secret of change is to focus all your energy, not on fighting the old, but on building the new."

- Socrates

52.

"Success is no accident. It is hard work, perseverance, learning, studying, sacrifice and most of all, love what you are doing or learning to do."

- Pele

53.

"The trouble is, you think you have time."

- Buddha

54.

"You can't let your failures define you. You have to let your failures teach you."

- Barack Obama

55.

"Stop being afraid of what could go wrong, and start being excited about what could go right."

- Tony Robbins

56.

"Defeat is a state of mind; no one is ever defeated until defeat is accepted as a reality."

- Bruce Lee

57.

"Our greatest glory is not in never falling, but in rising every time we fall."

- Confucius

58.

"Success is going from failure to failure without losing your enthusiasm."

- Winston Churchill

59.

"No matter what people tell you, words and ideas can the world."

- Robin Williams

60.

"Life is like riding a bicycle. To keep your balance, you must keep moving."

- Albert Einstein

61.

"Everything is hard before it is easy."

- Goethe

62.

"At the end of the day, we can endure much more than we think we can."

- Frida Kahlo

63.

"Either you run the day, or the day runs you."

- Jim Rohn

64.

"Only I can change my life. No one can do it for me."

- Carol Burnett

65.

"Very little is needed to make a happy life; it is all within yourself, in your way of thinking."

- Marcus Aurelius

66.

"The woman who follows the crowd will usually go no further than the crowd. The woman who walks alone is likely to find herself in places no one has been before."

- Albert Einstein

67.

"The capacity to learn is a gift; the ability to learn is a skill; the willingness to learn is a choice."

- Brian Herbert

68.

"Strength does not come from winning. Your struggles develop your strengths. When you go through hardships and decide not to surrender, that is strength."

- Arnold Schwarzenegger

69.

"A dream doesn't become reality through magic; it takes sweat, determination and hard work."

- Colin Powell

70.

"It's okay to be a glowstick: Sometimes we have to break before we shine."

- Jadah Sellner

71.

"Dwell on the beauty of life. Watch the stars and see yourself running with them."

- Marcus Aurelius

72.

"You were born to win, but to be a winner, you must plan to win, prepare to win, and expect to win."

- Zig Ziglar

73.

"Words can inspire, thoughts can provoke, but only action truly brings you closer to your dreams."

- Brad Sugars

74.

"Be yourself; everyone else is already taken."

- Oscar Wilde

75.

"No one can make you feel inferior without your consent."

- Eleanor Roosevelt

76.

"Imperfection is beauty, madness is genius, and it's better to be absolutely ridiculous than absolutely boring."

- Marilyn Monroe

77.

"There are only 2 ways to live your life. One is as though nothing is a miracle. The other is as though everything is a miracle."

- Albert Einstein

78.

"I have not failed. I've just found 10,000 ways that won't work."

- Thomas A. Edison

79.

"Yesterday is history, tomorrow is a mystery, today is a gift of God, which is why we call it the present."

- Bill Keane

80.

"Life isn't about finding yourself. Life is about creating yourself."

- George Bernard Shaw

81.

"What you're supposed to do when you don't like a thing is change it. If you can't change it, change the way you think about it. Don't complain."

- Maya Angelou

82.

"It's the possibility of having a dream come true that makes life interesting."

- Paulo Coelho

83.

"Nothing is impossible. The word itself says 'I'm possible'!"

- Audrey Hepburn

84.

"Happiness is not something ready-made. It comes from your own actions."

- Dalai Lama XIV

85.

"Whatever you are, be a good one."

- Abraham Lincoln

86.

"Creativity is intelligence having fun."

- Albert Einstein

87.

"Optimism is the one quality more associated with success and happiness than any other."

- Brian Tracy

88.

"What you get by achieving your goals is not as important as what you become by achieving your goals."

- Henry David Thoreau

89.

"Don't live the same year 75 times and call it a life."

- Robin Sharma

90.

"There is no way to happiness. Happiness is the way."

- Thich Nhat Hanh

91.

"Genius is 1% inspiration, and 99% perspiration."

- Thomas Edison

92.

"The grass is greener where you water it."

- Neil Barringham

93.

"Never give up on a dream just because of the time it will take to accomplish it. The time will pass anyway."

- Earl Nightingale

94.

"Instead of wondering when your next vacation is, maybe you should set up a life you don't need to escape from."

- Seth Godin

95.

"Sometimes you win, sometimes you learn."

- John Maxwell

96.

"What lies behind you and what lies in front of you, pales in comparison to what lies inside of you."

- Ralph Waldo Emerson

97.

"We know what we are, but not what we may be."

- William Shakespeare

98.

"Start by doing what's necessary; then do what's possible; and suddenly you are doing the impossible."

- Francis of Assisi

99.

"The measure of who we are is what we do with what we have."

- Vince Lombardi

100.

"We must let go of the life we have planned, so as to accept the one that is waiting for us."

- Joseph Campbell

101.

"There is nothing impossible to him who will try."

- Alexander the Great

102.

"Believe you can and you're halfway there."

- Theodore Roosevelt

103.

"If a man does not keep pace with his companions, perhaps it is because he hears a different drummer. Let him step to the music which he hears, however measured or far away."

- Henry David Thoreau

104.

"What we think, we become."

- Buddha

105.

"Cherish your visions and your dreams as they are the children of your soul, the blueprints of your ultimate achievements."

- Napoleon Hill

106.

"The best way out is always through."

- Robert Frost

107.

"Today is the only day. Yesterday is gone."

- John Wooden

108.

"Follow your bliss and the universe will open doors where there were only walls."

- Joseph Campbell

109.

"If you accept the expectations of others, especially negative ones, then you never will change the outcome."

- Michael Jordan

110.

"We can change our lives. We can do, have, and be exactly what we wish."

- Tony Robbins

111.

"Don't judge each day by the harvest you reap, but by the seeds that you plant."

- Robert Louis Stevenson

112.

"I believe that one defines oneself by reinvention. To not be like your parents. To not be like your friends. To be yourself. To cut yourself out of stone."

- Henry Rollins

113.

"Just don't give up trying to do what you really want to do. Where there is love and inspiration, I don't think you can go wrong."

- Ella Fitzgerald

114.

"One today is worth two tomorrows."

- Benjamin Franklin

115.

"To the mind that is still, the whole universe surrenders."

- Lao Tzu

116.

"Look within. Within is the fountain of good, and it will ever bubble up, if thou wilt ever dig."

- Marcus Aurelius

117.

"Your big opportunity may be right where you are now."

- Napoleon Hill

118.

"God loves to help him who strives to help himself."

- Aeschylus

119.

"Shoot for the moon, and if you miss you will still be among the stars."

- Les Brown

120.

"Belief creates the actual fact."

- William James

121.

"You are always free to change your mind and choose a different future, or a different past."

- Richard Bach

122.

"Most of us have far more courage than we ever dreamed we possessed."

- Dale Carnegie

123.

"Whoever is happy will make others happy too."

- Anne Frank

124.

"No act of kindness, no matter how small, is ever wasted."

- Aesop

125.

"The only journey is the one within."

-   Rainer Maria Rilke

126.

"It is in your moments of decision that your destiny is shaped."

-   Tony Robbins

127.

"What we achieve inwardly will change outer reality."

-   Plutarch

128.

"All you need is the plan, the road map, and the courage to press on to your destination."

- Earl Nightingale

129.

"Change your thoughts and you change your world."

- Norman Vincent Peale

130.

"The best preparation for tomorrow is doing your best today."

- H. Jackson Brown Jr.

131.

"Be faithful to that which exists within yourself."

- Andre Gide

132.

"You change your life by changing your heart."

- Max Lucado

133.

"The only way to discover the limits of the possible is to go beyond them into the impossible."

- Arthur C. Clarke

134.

"Out of difficulties grow miracles."

- Jean de la Bruyere

135.

"Happiness resides not in possessions, and not in gold; happiness dwells in the soul."

- Democritus

136.

"When you have a dream, you've got to grab it and never let go."

- Carol Burnett

137.

"Enthusiasm moves the world."

- Arthur Balfour

138.

"Try to be like the turtle – at ease in your own shell."

- Bill Copeland

139.

"Man never made any material as resilient as the human spirit."

- Bernard Williams

140.

"The pessimist sees difficulty in every opportunity. The optimist sees opportunity in every difficulty."

- Winston Churchill

141.

"Life is 10% what happens to us and 90% how we react to it."

- Dennis P. Kimbro

142.

"Be not afraid of life. Believe that life is worth living, and your belief will help create the fact."

- William James

143.

"Even if you're on the right track, you'll get run over if you just sit there."

- Will Rogers

144.

"Nurture your mind with great thoughts. To believe in the heroic makes heroes."

- Benjamin Disraeli

145.

"Luck is a dividend of sweat. The more you sweat, the luckier you get."

- Ray Kroc

146.

"When I let go of what I am, I become what I might be."

- Lao Tzu

147.

"The great thing in this world is not so much where you stand, as in what direction you are moving."

- Oliver Wendell Holmes

148.

"The difference between a successful person and others is not a lack of strength, not a lack of knowledge, but rather a lack of will."

- Vince Lombardi

149.

"If not us, who? If not now, when?"

- John F. Kennedy

150.

"Do not go where the path may lead, go where there is no path and leave a trail."

- Ralph Waldo Emerson

151.

"Every noble work is at first impossible."

- Thomas Carlyle

152.

"Nobody ever wrote down a plan to be broke, fat, lazy, or stupid. Those things are what happen when you don't have a plan."

- Larry Winget

153.

"Every strike brings me closer to the next home run."

- Babe Ruth

154.

"I am not a product of my circumstances. I am a product of my decisions."

- Stephen Covey

155.

"Eighty percent of success is showing up."

- Woody Allen

156.

"We become what we think about."

- Earl Nightingale

157.

"Life is about making an impact, not making an income."

- Kevin Kruse

158.

"You miss 100% of the shots you don't take."

- Wayne Gretzky

159.

"Definiteness of purpose is the starting point of all achievement."

- W. Clement Stone

160.

"Life is what happens to you while you're busy making other plans."

- John Lennon

161.

"An unexamined life is not worth living."

- Socrates

162.

"Your time is limited, so don't waste it living someone else's life."

- Steve Jobs

163.

"Winning isn't everything, but wanting to win is."

- Vince Lombardi

164.

"You can never cross the ocean until you have the courage to lose sight of the shore."

- Christopher Columbus

165.

"Whether you think you can, or you think you can't, you're right."

- Henry Ford

166.

"The two most important days in your life are the day you are born, and the day you find out why."

- Mark Twain

167.

"Life shrinks or expands in proportion to one's courage"

- Anais Nin

168.

"There is only one way to avoid criticism: do nothing, say nothing, and be nothing."

- Aristotle

169.

"Everything you've ever wanted is on the other side of fear."

- George Addair

170.

"When one door of happiness closes, another opens, but often we look so long at the closed door that we do not see the one that has been opened for us."

- Helen Keller

171.

"Everything has beauty, but not everyone can see."

- Confucius

172.

"Life is not measured by the number of breaths we take, but by the moments that take our breath away."

- Maya Angelou

173.

"I have been impressed with the urgency of doing. Knowing is not enough; we must apply. Being willing is not enough; we must do."

- Leonardo da Vinci

174.

"What's money? A man is a success if he gets up in the morning and goes to bed at night, and in between does what he wants to do."

- Bob Dylan

175.

"There are no traffic jams along the extra mile."

- Roger Staubach

176.

"I would rather die of passion than of boredom."

- Vincent van Gogh

177.

"Build your own dreams, or someone else will hire you to build theirs."

- Farrah Gray

178.

"Remember that not getting what you want is sometimes a wonderful stroke of luck."

- Dalai Lama

179.

"Dream big and dare to fail."

- Norman Vaughan

180.

"If you do what you've always done, you'll get what you've always gotten."

- Tony Robbins

181.

"It's your place in the world; it's your life. Go on and do all you can with it and make it the life you want to live."

- Mae Jemison

182.

"Life is what we make it. Always has been, always will be."

- Grandma Moses

183.

"When everything seems to be going against you, remember that the airplane takes off against the wind, not with it."

- Henry Ford

184.

"Either write something worth reading or do something worth writing."

- Benjamin Franklin

185.

"If you can dream it, you can achieve it."

- Zig Ziglar

186.

"Learn how to be happy with what you have while you pursue all that you want."

- Jim Rohn

187.

"There is no place so awake and alive as the edge of becoming."

- Sue Monk Kidd

188.

"I can't change the direction of the wind, but I can adjust my sails to always reach my destination."

- Jimmy Dean

189.

"The real opportunity for success lies within the person and not in the job."

- Zig Ziglar

190.

"You can't use up creativity. The more you use, the more you have."

- Maya Angelou

191.

"We can't help everyone, but everyone can help someone."

- Ronald Reagan

192.

"Whenever you see a successful person you only see the public glories, never the private sacrifices to reach them."

- Vaibhav Shah

193.

"Opportunities don't happen, you create them."

- Chris Grosser

194.

"If you don't value your time, neither will others. Stop giving away your time and talents – start charging for it."

- Kim Garst

195.

"A successful man is one who can lay a firm foundation with the bricks others have thrown at him."

- David Brinkley

196.

"What seems to us as bitter trials are often blessings in disguise."

- Oscar Wilde

197.

"The distance between insanity and genius is measured only by success."

- Bruce Feirstein

198.

"When you stop chasing the wrong things, you give the right things a chance to catch you."

- Lolly Daskal

199.

"I believe that the only courage anybody ever needs is the courage to follow your own dreams."

- Oprah Winfrey

200.

"Innovation distinguishes between a leader and a follower."

- Steve Jobs

201.

"There are two types of people who will tell you that you cannot make a difference in this world: those who are afraid to try, and those who are afraid you will succeed."

- Ray Goforth

202.

"Thinking should become your capital asset, no matter whatever ups and downs you come across in your life."

- A.P.J. Abdul Kalam

203.

"Success is the sum of small efforts, repeated day-in and day-out."

- Robert Collier

204.

"You may only succeed if you desire succeeding; you may only fail if you do not mind failing."

- Philippos

205.

"Courage is resistance to fear, mastery of fear – not absence of fear."

- Mark Twain

206.

"Only put off until tomorrow what you are willing to die having left undone."

- Pablo Picasso

207.

"We become what we think about most of the time, and that's the strangest secret."

- Earl Nightingale

208.

"The only place where success comes before work is in the dictionary."

- Vidal Sassoon

209.

"Success is liking yourself, liking what you do, and liking how you do it."

- Maya Angelou

210.

"The first step towards success is taken when you refuse to be a captive of the environment in which you first find yourself."

- Mark Caine

211.

"The successful warrior is the average man, with laser-like focus."

- Bruce Lee

212.

"Develop success from failures. Discouragement and failure are two of the surest stepping stones to success."

- Dale Carnegie

213.

"If you don't design your own life plan, chances are you'll fall into someone else's plan. And guess what they have planned for you? Not much.

- Jim Rohn

214.

"If you genuinely want something, don't wait for it – teach yourself to be impatient."

- Gurbaksh Chahal

215.

"Don't let the fear of losing be greater than the excitement of winning."

- Robert Kiyosaki

216.

"If you want to make a permanent change, stop focusing on the size of your problems and start focusing on the size of you!"

- T. Harv Eker

217.

"The number one reason people fail in life is because they listen to their friends, family, and neighbors."

- Napoleon Hill

218.

"The reason most people never reach their goals is that they don't define them, or ever seriously consider them as believable or achievable. Winners can tell you where they are going, what they plan to do along the way, and who will be sharing the adventure with them."

- Denis Waitley

219.

"In my experience, there is only one motivation, and that is desire. No reasons or principle contain it or stand against it."

- Jane Smiley

220.

"Success does not consist in never making mistakes, but in never making the same one a second time."

- George Bernard Shaw

221.

"You must expect great things of yourself before you can do them."

- Michael Jordan

222.

"Motivation is what gets you started. Habit is what keeps you going."

- Jim Ryun

223.

"People rarely succeed unless they have fun in what they are doing."

- Dale Carnegie

224.

"There is no chance, no destiny, no fate, that can hinder or control the firm resolve of a determined soul."

- Ella Wheeler Wilcox

225.

"Our greatest fear should not be of failure, but of succeeding at things in life that don't really matter."

- Francis Chan

226.

"You've got to get up every morning with determination if you're going to go to bed with satisfaction."

- George Lorimer

227.

"A goal is not always meant to be reached; it often serves simply as something to aim at."

- Bruce Lee

228.

"To accomplish great things, we must not only act, but also dream, not only plan, but also believe."

- Anatole France

229.

"Most of the important things in the world have been accomplished by people who have kept on trying when there seemed to be no help at all."

- Dale Carnegie

230.

"You measure the size of the accomplishment by the obstacles you had to overcome to reach your goals."

- Booker T. Washington

231.

"Real difficulties can be overcome; it is only the imaginary ones that are unconquerable."

- Theodore N. Vail

232.

"It is better to fail in originality than to succeed in imitation."

- Herman Melville

233.

"Little minds are tamed and subdued by misfortune; but great minds rise above it."

- Washington Irving

234.

"Failure is the condiment that gives success its flavor."

- Truman Capote

235.

"Don't let what you cannot do interfere with what you can do."

- John R. Wooden

236.

"You may have to fight a battle more than once to win it."

- Margaret Thatcher

237.

"A man can be as great as he wants to be. If you believe in yourself and have the courage, the determination, the dedication, the competitive drive and if you are willing to sacrifice the little things in life and pay the price for things that are worthwhile, it can be done."

- Vince Lombardi

238.

"The most common way people give up their power is by thinking they don't have any."

- Alice Walker

239.

"Believe in yourself! Have faith in your abilities! Without a humble but reasonable confidence in your own powers, you cannot be successful or happy."

- Norman Vincent Peale

240.

"Do not wait; the time will never be 'just right.' Start where you stand, and work with whatever tools you may have at your command, and better tools will be found as you go along."

- George Herbert

241.

"The most difficult thing is the decision to act, the rest is merely tenacity."

- Amelia Earhart

242.

"Press forward. Do not stop, do not linger in your journey, but strive for the mark set before you."

- George Whitefield

243.

"There will be obstacles. There will be doubters. There will be mistakes. But with hard work, there are no limits."

- Michael Phelps

244.

"You just can't beat the person who never gives up."

- Babe Ruth

245.

"Many of life's failures are people who did not realize how close they were to success when they gave up."

- Thomas A. Edison

246.

"With the new day comes new strength and new thoughts."

- Eleanor Roosevelt

247.

"Failure will never overtake me if my determination to succeed is strong enough."

- Og Mandino

248.

"Always wake up with a smile knowing that today you are going to have fun accomplishing what others are too afraid to do."

- Mark Cuban

249.

"Nothing happens to you; it happens for you. See the positive in negative events."

- Joel Osteen

250.

"Every problem is a gift – without problems we would not grow."

- Tony Robbins

251.

"Without passion, you don't have energy. Without energy, you have nothing."

- Warren Buffett

252.

"We define ourselves far too often by our past failures. That's not you. You are this person right now. You're the person who has learned from those failures."

- Joe Rogan

253.

"Work like there is someone working 24 hours a day to take it all away from you."

- Mark Cuban

254.

"As soon as something stops being fun, I think it's time to move on. Life is too short to be unhappy. Waking up stressed and miserable is not a good way to live."

- Sir Richard Branson

255.

"Everything is either an opportunity to grow or an obstacle to keep you from growing. You get to choose."

- Wayne Dyer

256.

"Hardships often prepare ordinary people for an extraordinary destiny."

- C.S. Lewis

257.

"There is only one thing that makes a dream impossible to achieve: the fear of failure."

- Paulo Coelho

258.

"If you can tune into your purpose and really align with it, setting goals so that your vision is an expression of that purpose, then life flows much more easily."

- Jack Canfield

259.

"Believe in yourself, take on your challenges, dig deep within yourself to conquer fears. Never let anyone bring you down. You got to keep going."

- Chantal Sutherland

260.

"If you can't, you must. If you must, you can."

- Tony Robbins

261.

"It's not about perfect. It's about effort. And when you bring that effort every single day, that's where transformation happens. That's how change occurs."

- Jillian Michaels

262.

"Hard times don't create heroes. It is during the hard times when the 'hero' within us is revealed."

- Bob Riley

263.

"If you set goals and go after them with all the determination you can muster, your gifts will take you places that will amaze you."

- Les Brown

264.

"Believe in yourself. You are braver than you think, more talented than you know, and capable of more than you imagine."

- Roy T. Bennett

265.

"Strength does not come from physical capacity. It comes from an indomitable will."

- Mahatma Gandhi

266.

"Life is not about waiting for the storm to pass but learning to dance in the rain."

- Vivian Greene

267.

"You will never find time for anything. If you want time, you must make it."

- Charles Buxton

268.

"The best way to gain self-confidence is to do what you are afraid to do."

- Swati Sharma

269.

"Fortune always favors the brave, and never helps a man who does not help himself."

- P.T. Barnum

270.

"We don't develop courage by being happy every day. We develop it by surviving difficult times and challenging adversity."

- Barbara De Angelis

271.

"When something is important enough, you do it even if the odds are not in your favor."

- Elon Musk

272.

"By recording your dreams and goals on paper, you set in motion the process of becoming the person you most want to be. Put your future in good hands – your own."

- Mark Victor Hansen

273.

"The man who moves a mountain begins by carrying away small stones."

- Confucius

274.

"You can conquer almost any fear if you will only make up your mind to do so. For remember, fear doesn't exist anywhere except in the mind."

- Dale Carnegie

275.

"Limitations live only in our minds. But if we use our imaginations, our possibilities become limitless."

-   Jamie Paolinetti

276.

"Challenges are what make life interesting and overcoming them is what makes life meaningful."

-   Joshua Marine

277.

"Learn from the past, set vivid, detailed goals for the future, and live in the only moment of time over which you have any control: now."

-   Denis Waitley

278.

"Only those who dare to fail greatly can ever achieve greatly."

- Robert F. Kennedy

279.

"Happiness is letting go of what you think your life is supposed to look like and enjoying it for everything that it is."

- Mandy Hale

280.

"Concentrate all your thoughts upon the work in hand. The sun's rays do not burn until brought to a focus."

- Alexander Graham Bell

281.

"Opportunity is missed by most people because it is dressed in overalls and looks like hard work."

- Thomas Edison

282.

"Just one small positive thought in the morning can change your whole day."

- Dalai Lama

283.

"Time is an equal opportunity employer. Each human being has exactly the same number of hours and minutes every day. Rich people can't buy more hours. Scientists can't invent new minutes. And you can't save time to spend it on another day. Even so, time is amazingly fair and forgiving. No matter how much time you've wasted in the past, you still have an entire tomorrow."

- Denis Waitley

284.

"Do the hard jobs first. The easy jobs will take care of themselves."

- Dale Carnegie

285.

"Developing a good work ethic is key. Apply yourself at whatever you do, whether you're a janitor or taking your first summer job because that work ethic will be reflected in everything you do in life."

- Tyler Perry

286.

"Happiness is not in the mere possession of money; it lies in the joy of achievement, in the thrill of creative effort."

- Franklin D. Roosevelt

287.

"Success means doing the best with what we have. Success is the doing, not the getting; in the trying, not the triumph. Success is a personal standard, reaching for the highest that is in us, becoming all that we can be."

- Zig Ziglar

288.

"Do more than is required. What is the distance between someone who achieves their goals consistently and those who spend their lives and careers merely following? The extra mile."

- Gary Ryan Blair

289.

"Things may come to those who wait, but only the things left by those who hustle."

- Abraham Lincoln

290.

"To think too long about a thing often becomes its undoing."

- Eva Young

291.

"Don't be afraid to give your best to what seemingly are small jobs. Every time you conquer one it makes you that much stronger. If you do the little jobs well, the big ones will tend to take care of themselves."

- William Patten

292.

"Talent means nothing, while experience, acquired in humility and with hard work, means everything."

- Patrick Suskind

293.

"Success seems to be connected with action. Successful people keep moving. They make mistakes, but they don't quit."

- Conrad Hilton

294.

"You don't have to see the whole staircase, just take the first step."

- Martin Luther King, Jr.

295.

"This is the real secret of life – to be completely engaged with what you are doing in the here and now. And instead of calling it work, realize it is play."

- Alan Watts

296.

"Motivation is a fire from within. If someone else tries to light that fire under you, chances are it will burn very briefly."

- Stephen R. Covey

297.

"Happiness is the real sense of fulfilment that comes from hard work."

- Joseph Barbara

298.

"If I had eight hours to chop down a tree, I'd spend six hours sharpening my axe."

- Abraham Lincoln

299.

"Nothing is less productive than to make more efficient what should not be done at all."

- Peter Drucker

300.

"Let me tell you the secret that has led to my goals: my strength lies solely in my tenacity."

- Louis Pasteur

301.

"Luck is a matter of preparation meeting opportunity."

- Seneca

302.

"It is not a daily increase, but a daily decrease. Hack away at the inessentials."

- Bruce Lee

303.

"If you want to make an easy job seem mighty hard, just keep putting off doing it."

- Olin Miller

304.

"Attitude is a choice. Happiness is a choice. Optimism is a choice. Kindness is a choice. Giving is a choice. Respect is a choice. Whatever choice you make, makes you. Choose wisely."

- Roy T. Bennett

305.

"Amateurs sit and wait for inspiration, the rest of us just get up and go to work."

- Stephen King

306.

"There are no shortcuts to any place worth going."

- Beverly Sills

307.

"If something is wrong, fix it now. But train yourself not to worry, worry fixes nothing."

- Ernest Hemingway

308.

"Much of the stress that people feel doesn't come from having too much to do. It comes from not finishing what they started."

- David Allen

309.

"Whatever you do, do it with all your might. Work at it, early and late, in season and out of season, not leaving a stone unturned, and never deferring for a single hour that which can be done just as well as now."

- Margaret Fuller

310.

"It isn't the mountains ahead to climb that wear you out; it's the pebble in your shoe."

- Muhammad Ali

311.

"Your ability to discipline yourself to set clear goals, and then to work toward them every day, will do more to guarantee your success than any other single factor."

- Brian Tracy

312.

"Follow effective actions with quiet reflection. From the quiet reflection will come even more effective action."

- Peter Drucker

313.

"You can't change how people treat you or what they say about you. All you can do is change how you react to it."

- Mahatma Gandhi

314.

"Do not be embarrassed by your failures, learn from them and start again."

- Sir Richard Branson

315.

"I have always believed, and I still believe, that whatever good or bad fortune may come our way we can always give it meaning and transform it into something of value."

- Hermann Hesse

316.

"There are two primary choices in life: to accept conditions as they exist, or accept the responsibility for changing them."

- Denis Waitley

317.

"As long as they are well-intentioned, mistakes are not a matter for shame, but for learning."

- Margaret Heffernan

318.

"Show me a person who has never made a mistake and I'll show you someone who has never achieved much."

- Joan Collins

319.

"You are never too old to set another goal or to dream a new dream."

- C.S. Lewis

320.

"The only thing that overcomes hard luck is hard work."

- Harry Golden

321.

"Some people look for a beautiful place. Others make a place beautiful."

- Hazrat Inayat Khan

322.

"My mission in life is not merely to survive, but to thrive."

- Maya Angelou

323.

"You are enough just as you are."

- Meghan Markle

324.

"The bad news is time flies. The good news is you're the pilot."

- Michael Altshuler

325.

"You make a life out of what you have, not what you're missing."

- Kate Morton

326.

"You cannot change what you are, only what you do."

- Philip Pullman

327.

"It is not enough to have a good mind; the important thing is to use it well."

- Rene Descartes

328.

"People begin to become successful the minute they decide to be."

- Harvey Mackay

329.

"Walk to your goal firmly and with bold steps."

- Kahlil Gibran

330.

"Lay plans for something big by starting with it when small."

- Lao Tzu

331.

"One's destination is never a place, but a new way of seeing things."

- Henry Miller

332.

"It's how you deal with failure that determines how you achieve success."

- David Feherty

333.

"It takes as much energy to wish as it does to plan."

- Eleanor Roosevelt

334.

"Do anything, but let it produce joy."

- Walt Whitman

335.

"Do your little bit of good where you are; it's those little bits of good put together that overwhelm the world."

- Desmond Tutu

336.

"No one is useless in this world who lightens the burdens of another."

- Charles Dickens

337.

"As we work to create light for others, we naturally light our own way."

- Mary Anne Radmacher

338.

"Dwell on the beauty of life. Watch the stars, and see yourself running with them."

- Marcus Aurelius

339.

"I believe great people do things before they are ready."

- Amy Poehler

340.

"I have discovered in life that there are ways of getting almost anywhere you want to go, if you really want to go."

- Langston Hughes

341.

"If you spend too much time thinking about a thing, you'll never get it done."

- Bruce Lee

342.

"For me, becoming isn't about arriving somewhere or achieving a certain aim. I see it instead as forward motion, a means of evolving, a way to reach continuously toward a better self. The journey doesn't end."

- Michelle Obama

343.

"You are the one that possesses the keys to your being. You carry the passport to your own happiness."

- Diane von Furstenberg

344.

"We do not need magic to change the world, we carry all the power we need inside ourselves already: we have the power to imagine better."

- J.K. Rowling

345.

"Take your victories, whatever they may be, cherish them, use them, but don't settle for them."

- Mia Hamm

346.

"If you're going to try, go all the way. There is no other feeling like that. You will be alone with the gods, and the nights will flame with fire. You will ride life straight to perfect laughter. It's the only good fight there is."

- Charles Bukowski

347.

"Change the world by being yourself."

- Amy Poehler

348.

"All limitations are self-imposed."

- Oliver Wendell Holmes

349.

"Problems are not stop signs, they are guidelines."

- Robert H. Schiuller

350.

"One day, the people that don't even believe in you will tell everyone how they met you."

- Johnny Depp

351.

"Have enough courage to start and enough heart to finish."

- Jessica N.S. Yourko

352.

"Hate comes from intimidation, love comes from appreciation."

- Tyga

353.

"Determine your priorities and focus on them."

- Eileen McDargh

354.

"Dream as if you'll live forever, live as if you'll die today."

- James Dean

355.

"There is no substitute for hard work."

- Thomas Edison

356.

"Let the beauty of what you love be what you do."

- Rumi

357.

"May your choices reflect your hopes, not your fears."

- Nelson Mandela

358.

"A happy soul is the best shield for a cruel world."

- Atticus

359.

"Life becomes easier when you learn to accept the apology never got."

- R. Brault

360.

"Happiness depends upon ourselves."

- Aristotle

361.

"The meaning of life is to give life meaning."

- Ken Hudgins

362.

"The true meaning of life is to plant trees, under whose shade you do not expect to sit."

- Nelson Henderson

363.

"Embrace the glorious mess that you are."

- Elizabeth Gilbert

364.

"Normality is a paved road: it's comfortable to walk, but no flowers grow."

- Vincent van Gogh

365.

"Nothing lasts forever. Not even your troubles."

- Arnold H. Glasgow

Conclusion

Thanks again for choosing this book!

I hope you enjoyed the valuable motivation and inspiration that these quotes provide. Continue to look back at this book whenever you need a dose of inspiration to guide you!

If you enjoyed this book, I'd greatly appreciate it if you shared it with a friend and take the time to invite some inspiration into the life of others!